150 fun things to DOODLE

An interactive adventure in drawing lively animals, quirky robots, and zany doodads

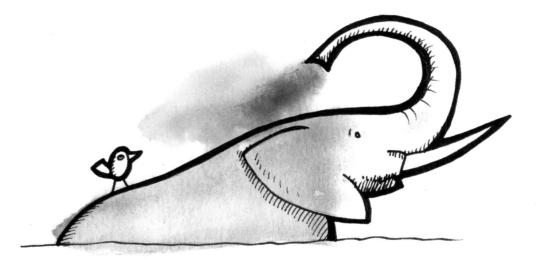

Walter Foster Jr.

www.walterfoster.com

Walter Foster Jr.,
an imprint of Quarto Publishing Group USA Inc.
3 Wrigley, Suite A
Irvine, CA 92618

Artwork © 2014 Green Android, Ltd.
Illustrated by Fiona Gowen
Photographs © Shutterstock
Written by Jennifer Gaudet

Publisher: Rebecca J. Razo
Art Director: Shelley Baugh
Project Editor: Jennifer Gaudet
Senior Editor: Stephanie Meissner
Assistant Editor: Janessa Osle
Production Designers: Debbie Aiken, Amanda Tannen
Production Manager: Nicole Szawlowski
Production Coordinator: Lawrence Marquez

3 5 7 9 10 8 6 4 2

table of contents

introduction to doodling

Welcome to your personal doodle journal! 150 Fun Things to Doodle is packed with animals, objects, gadgets, and machines for you to turn into fun and funky doodles, right on the pages of this book. Anything you can imagine—or see with your own eyes—can be doodled! If you've never doodled before, don't worry; doodling is simple, sometimes silly, and easy to learn. Your imagination, creativity, and drawing pencils can take you anywhere you like—and introduce you to zany friends and cool critters along the way. Most of all, you'll learn that fun doodle subjects are all around in our crazy, colorful world. All you need to do is bring your imagination along for the ride!

basic tools & materials

You can start every doodle with a drawing pencil. Then use markers, colored pencils, or even paint to add color!

drawing pencil
and paper

eraser

sharpener

colored
pencils

felt-tip markers

paintbrushes
& paints

how to use this book

Each section of this book begins with fun ideas and examples to inspire you. You'll find all kinds of step-by-step projects that begin with a few simple lines. Then a variety of prompts will inspire you to take your doodles to the next level by transforming them into exciting scenes!

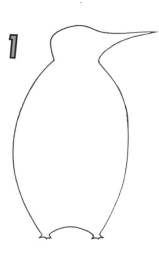

1

First draw the basic outline, using light lines.

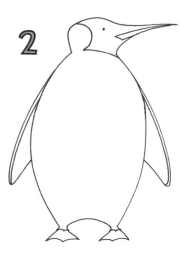

2

Continue to draw in the details.

3

Now darken the lines you will use for shaded areas.

4

Use your favorite art tool to add color!

warming up

Look closely at the doodles in this book, and you'll notice that they're made up of basic shapes, such as circles, triangles, and rectangles. Nearly anything you draw can begin with a simple shape!

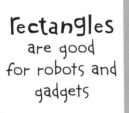

circles are perfect for clocks and fruit

rectangles are good for robots and gadgets

other simple shapes

Clouds are easy to draw, and they make good backgrounds. No two clouds need to look exactly alike!

grow a doodle

Continue simple doodles like this by "growing" them across your page. Then add leaves and flowers for extra detail.

Before you begin, warm up your hand by drawing squiggles and shapes.

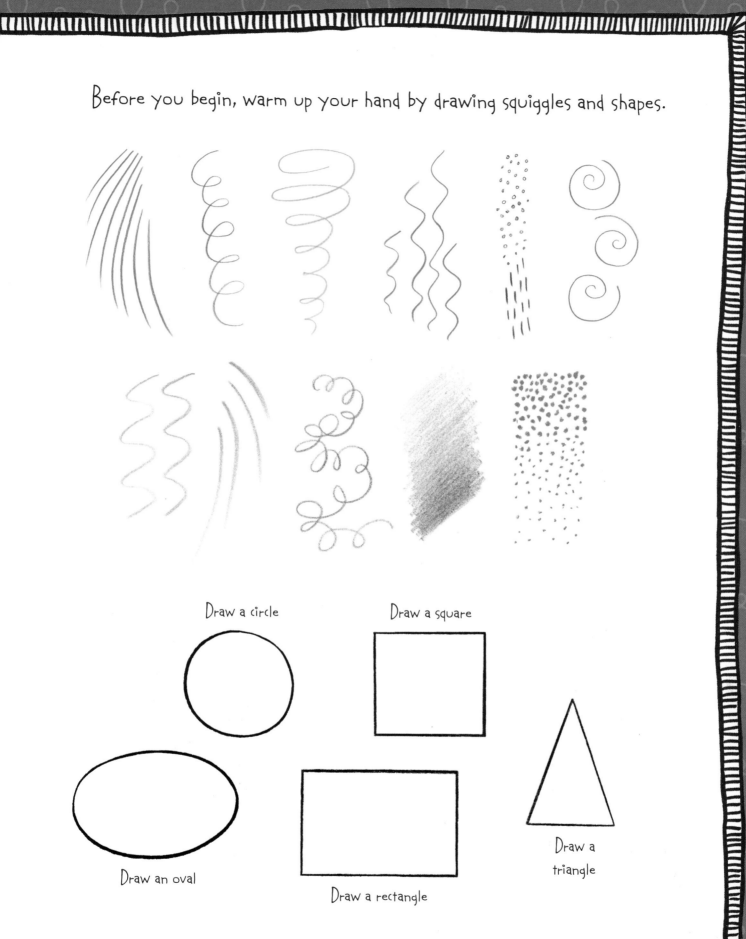

Draw a circle

Draw a square

Draw an oval

Draw a rectangle

Draw a triangle

exotic animals

Some of the most unique-looking animals on the planet live in wild jungles and forests. In this section you can bring them all to life right on the page. A world of exciting animal doodles awaits—including a zebra, a giraffe, and a big gray elephant!

zebra

giraffes

impala

elephant

tiger

giraffe

Giraffes are the tallest land animals in the world! They use their long necks to reach up high for leaves to eat. Doodle some trees near your giraffe so he has plenty to munch on!

doodle here!

elephant

Elephants are giants among the grasslands, forests, deserts, and mountains where they live. They travel in large groups, or herds. Why not draw an entire family on the opposite page?

doodle here!

tiger

One of the largest cats around, tigers are found in South and Southeast Asia. Have fun with the patterns on your tiger's coat—draw small triangles, dots, and blocks between his stripes!

doodled safari

Create a safari adventure with the animals you just learned to draw.
Don't forget to add trees, water, and bushes!

doodle here!

SECTION TWO
things that swim

The ocean is a very colorful place! There is so much we can't usually see from above the water. In this section you will doodle your way through an underwater world filled with swimming creatures, such as fish, sharks, whales, and more!

jellyfish

red gunard

krill

sea dragon

carp

octopus

pilot fish

harlequin
sweetlips

butterfly
fish

whale shark

hatchetfish

red gunard fish

This fish has a long, thin body and a curved face. Make sure you add small, short lines on the fins and tail and tiny dots all over the body.

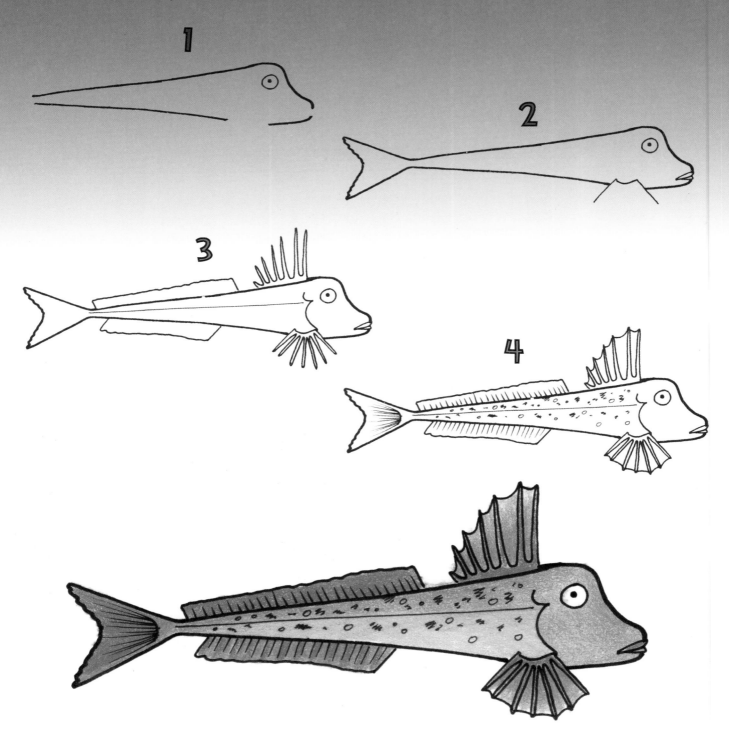

doodle here!

doodle here!

whale shark

Sharks are one of the most feared ocean animals. Good thing this one is a little more friendly. Feel free to make yours as fierce-looking as you like!

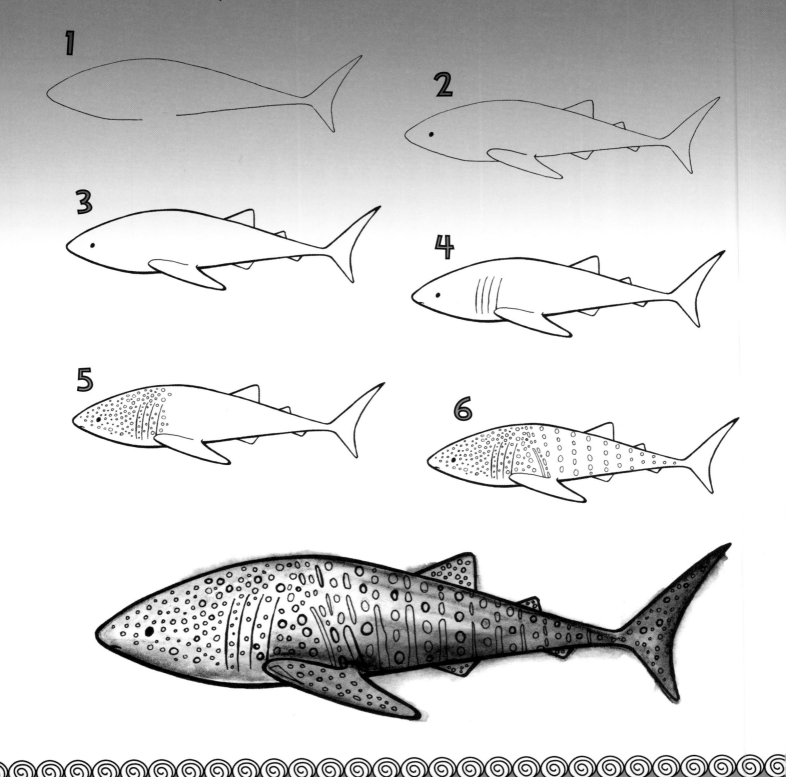

doodle here!

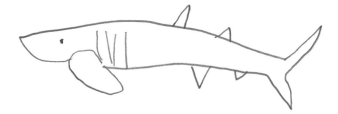

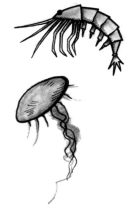

what's under the sea?

Fish and ocean critters come in all sorts of shapes, sizes, colors, and patterns!
How many different ones can you draw to fill this underwater world?
Look back to pages 20-21 for ideas.

doodle here!

27

polar animals

Penguins, polar bears, and several types of whales also swim, but in icy Arctic and Antarctic waters! Even the Arctic hare can swim across small streams. Practice doodling these polar creatures in their frozen habitat.

emperor penguin

walrus

narwhal

gull

Arctic hare

polar bear

minke whale

29

penguin

Penguins are perfectly at home sliding and swimming around in icy climates. They also love to dive into the water to catch fish! Can you think of a name for your penguin?

doodle here!

arctic adventure

Using as many of the icy critters on pages 28-29 as you can, fill these pages with your own creative, chilly scene!

doodle here!

things that crawl

In this section you will learn how to make all kinds of creatures crawl, climb, jump, and slither their way across the page! Many insects walk (or crawl), fly, and even swim, while amphibians and reptiles are impressive jumpers and climbers. What kinds of crazy, creepy crawlies can you come up with?

weevil

blister beetle

leaf insect

brown tree snake

grasshopper

giraffe-necked weevil

tortoise beetle

flying dragon

lantern bug

35

praying mantis

The praying mantis can turn its head nearly 180 degrees to spot prey. It is also a master of disguise! Can you draw yours surrounded by lots of green leaves, so that no one can find him?

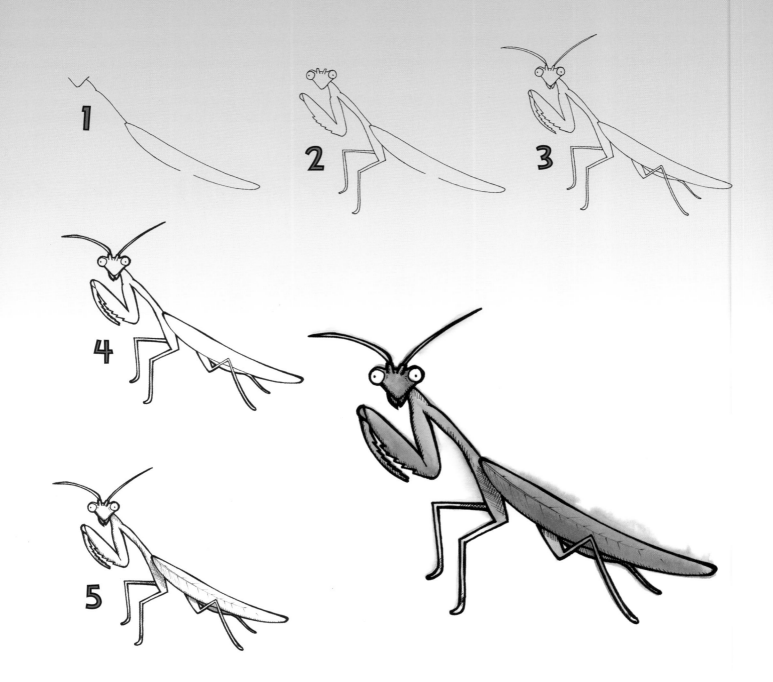

doodle here!

insect hunt

Our creepy-crawly friends are playing hide-and-seek!
Doodle the bugs you might find in this field inside each magnifying lens.

doodle here!

spikes, stripes, & spots

There are so many patterns to experiment with on these frogs, lizards, and snakes. Using the animals shown here as inspiration, fill your doodled creatures with dots, wavy lines, triangles, stripes, and more!

white-lipped tree frog

Parson's chameleon

frill-necked lizard

blue
poison
dart frog

flying dragon

brown tree snake

Amazon tree boa

green
tree frog

cylindrical
skink

Madagascar
day gecko

red-eyed tree frog

This little frog lives in the rainforest, surrounded by vibrant colors.
Experiment with bright shades of green, red, yellow, blue, and more!
Then add fun shapes, such as circles for the toes, triangles along the belly,
and a tiny diamond in the center of the eye.

doodle here!

green iguana

The green iguana has a lot more going on than just the color of its body. This large lizard has crazy textures, including a spiky spine, a striped tail, and a colorful flap of skin underneath its jaw!

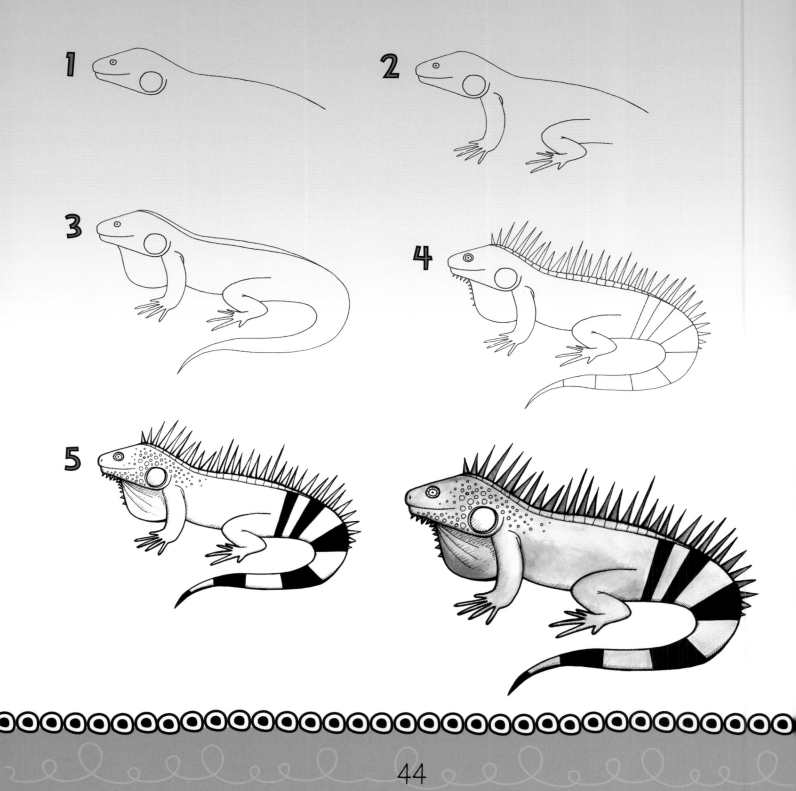

doodle here!

snake

This slithery reptile is all coiled up, so you can see the lines along its body that crisscross over one another. Where will your snake slide off to next?

doodle here!

hiding out

With so many leaves, trees, and plants around, crawling creatures have plenty of places to hide. Fill these pages with frogs, lizards, and snakes. You can even doodle more plants or trees!

doodle here!

things that fly

From delicate butterflies to a range of colorful birds, this section is filled with creatures in flight. The doodled sky is the limit—just make sure nobody accidentally flutters off the page!

blue morpho

Ashworth's rustic

monarch butterfly

great horned owl

peacock butterfly

common blue
butterfly

mountain ringlet

pebble prominent

hummingbird

cockatoo

painted lady
butterfly

This beautiful butterfly has bright colors that really "pop" against its black wings. Learn how to doodle your butterfly, and then set it free to fly around in an outdoor scene!

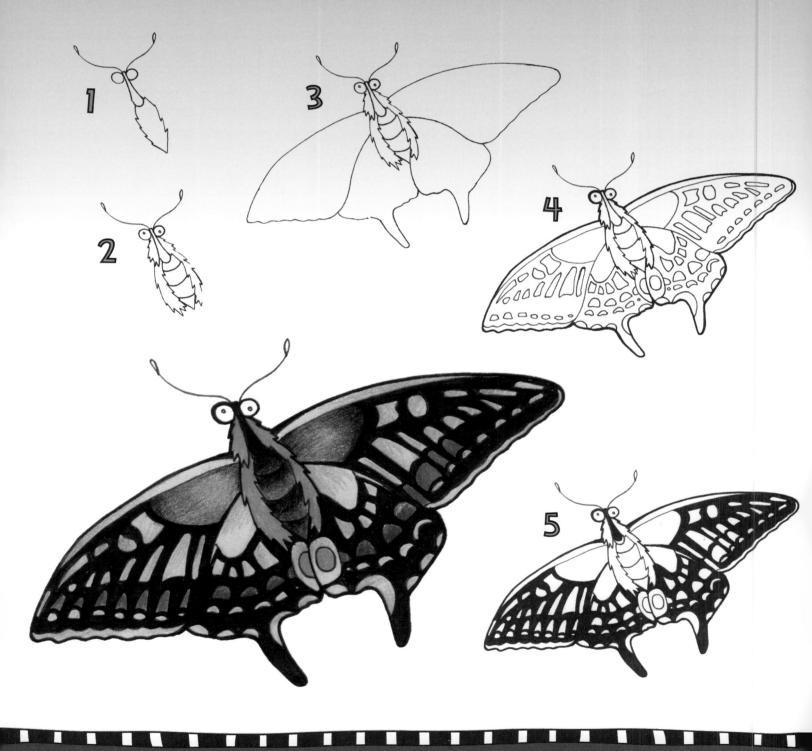

doodle
here!

flutter & fly

Now that you've seen the wide variety of colors and patterns a doodled butterfly can have, design your own using these templates!

doodle here!

hawk-headed parrot

Hawk-headed parrots live in the Amazon rainforests, but yours can come to life right here! This bird wears a red "crown" that looks like a real fan on top of its head. How many different colors can you include in your parrot?

doodle here!

great horned owl

With tiny diamond shapes, small dots, and a ring of stripes around its face, this owl is quite a hoot! Have fun filling in all of the tiny patterns on yours.

doodle here!

birds & branches

Some of these birds have fluffy feathers, while others have funny beaks!
No matter the bird, each one needs a safe place to land.
Which ones are perched on your branches?

flying lessons

Fill this big, blue sky with your favorite winged animals. Ready, set, fly!

doodle here!

fluffy friends

In this section you will create doodled versions of your favorite fluffy friends. Do any of these animals resemble a real pet that you have? Use your imagination and fill your practice pages with fun adventures for these loveable animals!

gerbil

guinea pig

old English sheepdog

rabbit

ferret

hamster

cat

pug

sheepdog

When doodling a sheepdog, the shaggier the better! Add wavy lines for the dog's furry body. Use close sections of short lines to create shading.

doodle here!

Pet accessories

Fluffy friends need toys to play with, and these pets have lost theirs! Can you help? Doodle a toy or other item for each of the pets below.

doodle here!

what's your pet thinking?

This is one hungry hamster! He's stuffing his cheeks with treats. What is he thinking about eating next? Fill in the thought bubble with your yummy ideas!

Color this cat with any colors you want. Then fill in her thought bubble!
What kind of mood is kitty in? Is she feeling mischievous, playful, or excited?
You decide!

things from science & space

There are all kinds of wacky, zany doodads in this section. You'll doodle your way through space exploration and crazy science lab concoctions—you'll even design your own personal robots. The quirkier the better—make it silly and have fun!

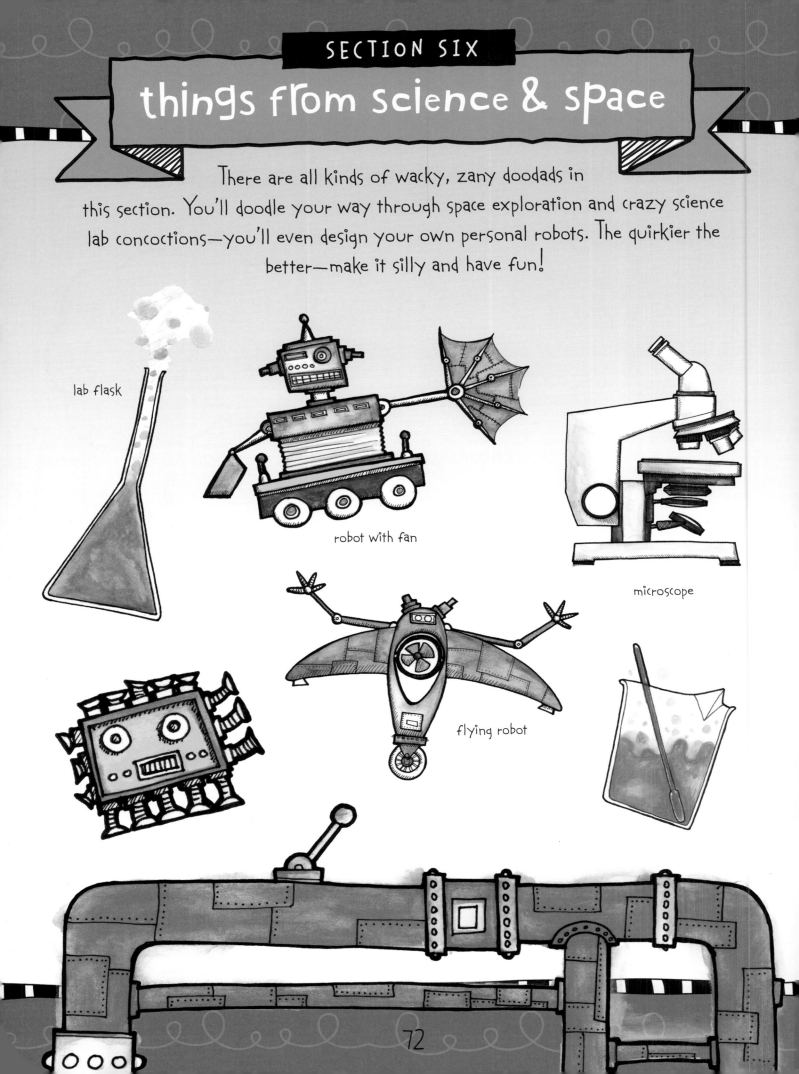

lab flask

robot with fan

microscope

flying robot

72

wheely robot

measuring cylinder

funnel

telescope

safety goggles

wheely robot

Robots with wheels can do lots of different jobs because they can move so fast! This wheely robot is made with stacked metal layers. When you finish your doodle, shade in a few shadows to give your robot a metallic look.

doodle here!

2015
2-14-15

Happy
valentines day

build your own robot

You can mix and match body parts to create tons of unique robots. Use the diagram below as a guide!

head

arm

body

legs and feet

Design your own robot in the space below. What job would you give it to do?
Maybe it could clean your room or make delicious snacks?
Don't forget to add legs and wheels so it can get around!

My robot's name is: _____.

telescope

Telescopes allow us to look into the night sky and discover amazing things our eyes cannot see on their own, such as stars, planets, and the solar system! Think about what you would explore as you draw this telescope.

doodle here!

doodled galaxy

Imagine looking at the galaxy through this telescope. What do you see? Doodle planets, stars, aliens, or even a spaceship!

doodle here!

science lab

This science lab is for creating fun doodled experiments! Playing with colors and chemistry can produce some pretty wacky results. Check out all the tools below. What crazy concoction can you mix up? Doodle your experiment on the next page.

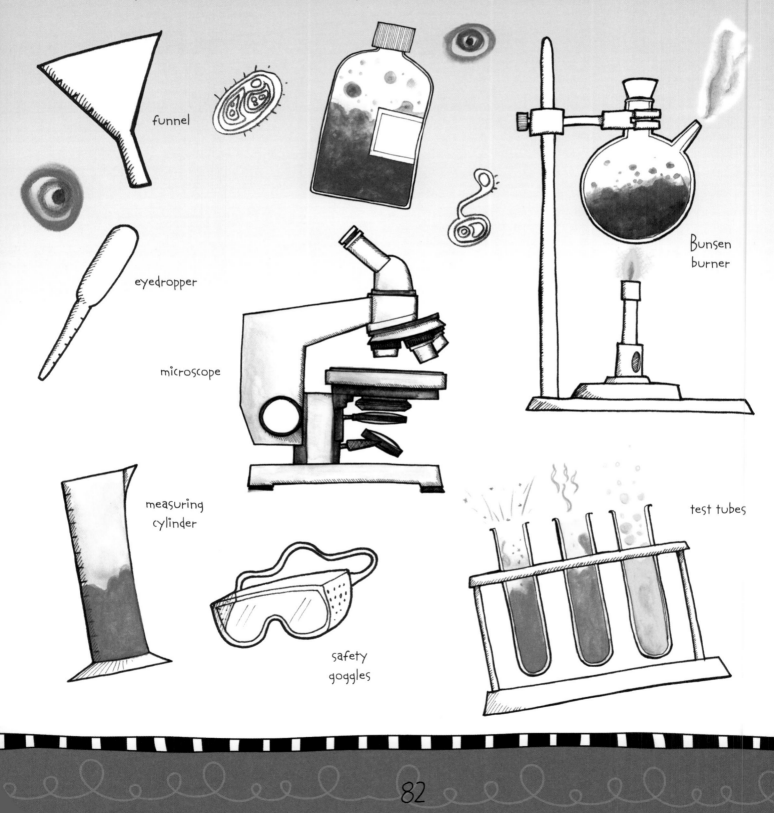

funnel

eyedropper

microscope

measuring cylinder

safety goggles

Bunsen burner

test tubes

doodle here!

microscope

Get a close-up peek at living organisms through the lens of your microscope. You never know what you might discover! Be sure to draw each knob and viewing lens just right.

What do you see
when you look through your
microscope? Imagine how the details,
lines, and patterns of your chosen
objects might look through a
super-magnified lens.
Doodle them below.

doodle here!

things that build & find

In this section you'll doodle objects and tools you might find at a construction site—cranes, drills, shovels, and other gadgets that help make super tall buildings. After that, you'll be back on the ground, hunting for buried treasure!

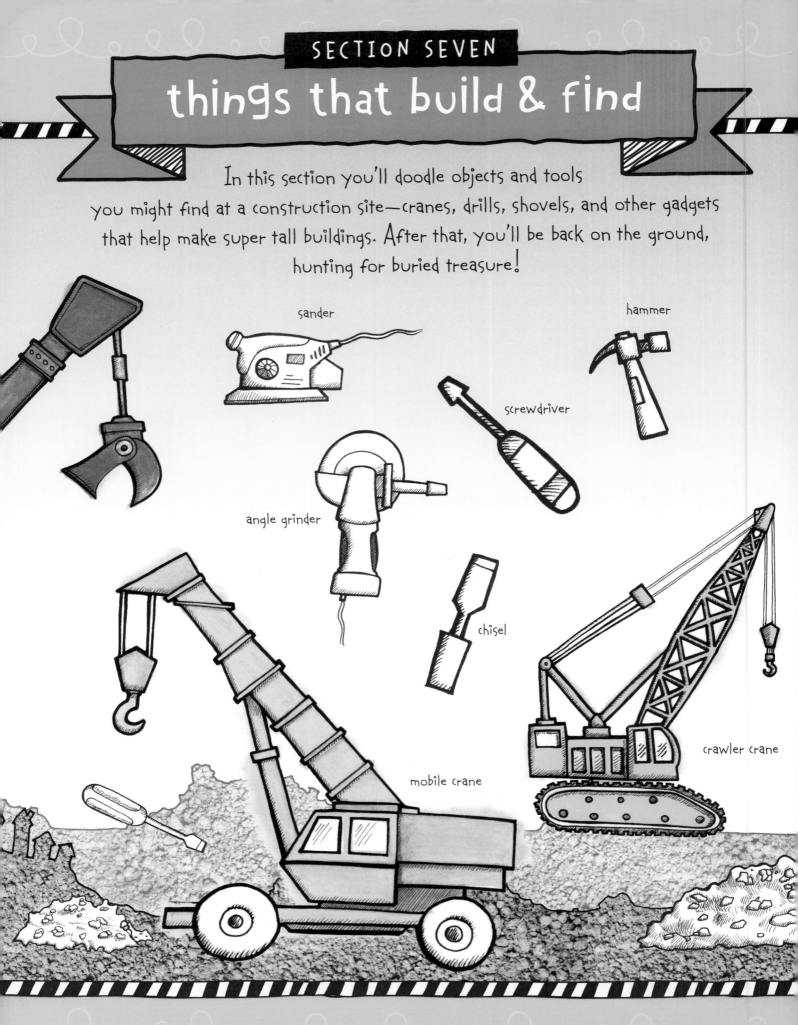

sander

hammer

screwdriver

angle grinder

chisel

mobile crane

crawler crane

orbital sander

jigsaw

wrench

leaf blower

drill

Power tools are helpful for making all kinds of things, from large to small. Can you think of some things you could make with this drill?

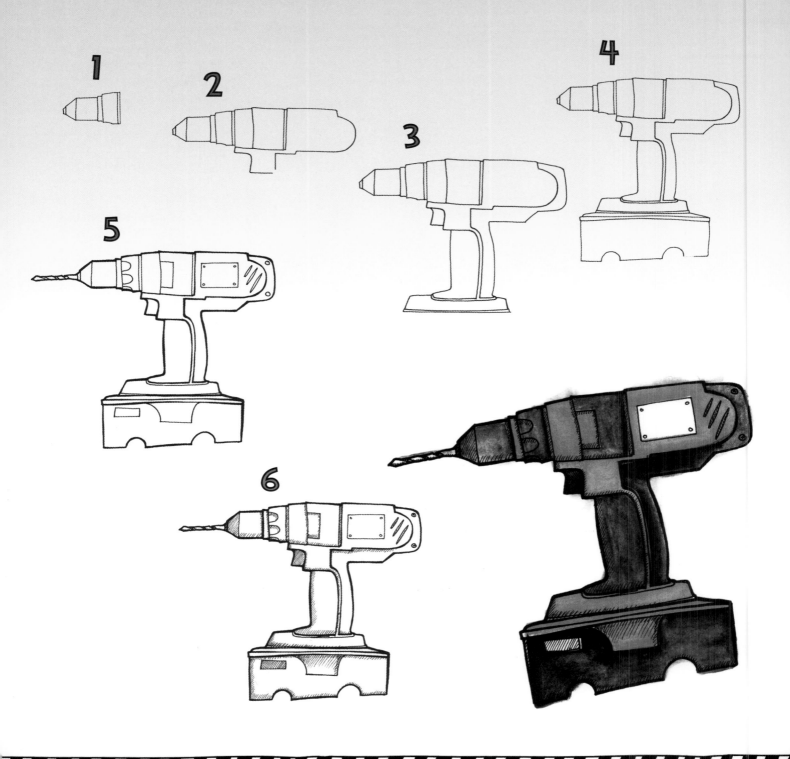

doodle here!

tool time

Imagine you have your very own workshop filled with tools.
Practice doodling your power tools, and then decide what you want to work on.
Are you building a treehouse? Or maybe fixing a broken toy?
You decide—fill these pages with your projects!

sander

screwdriver

circular saw

blowtorch

ruler

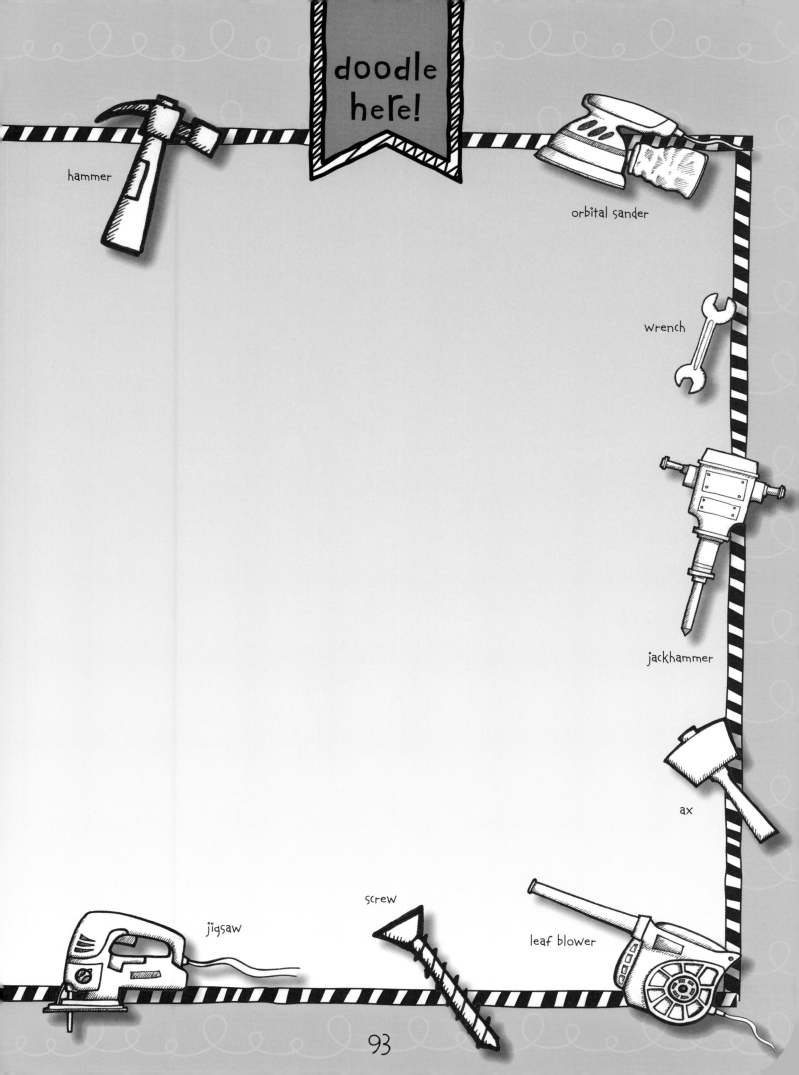

doodle here!

hammer

orbital sander

wrench

jackhammer

ax

jigsaw

screw

leaf blower

crane

Construction sites are busy, noisy places filled with crazy machines that reach up into the sky. What kinds of cool structures would you build?

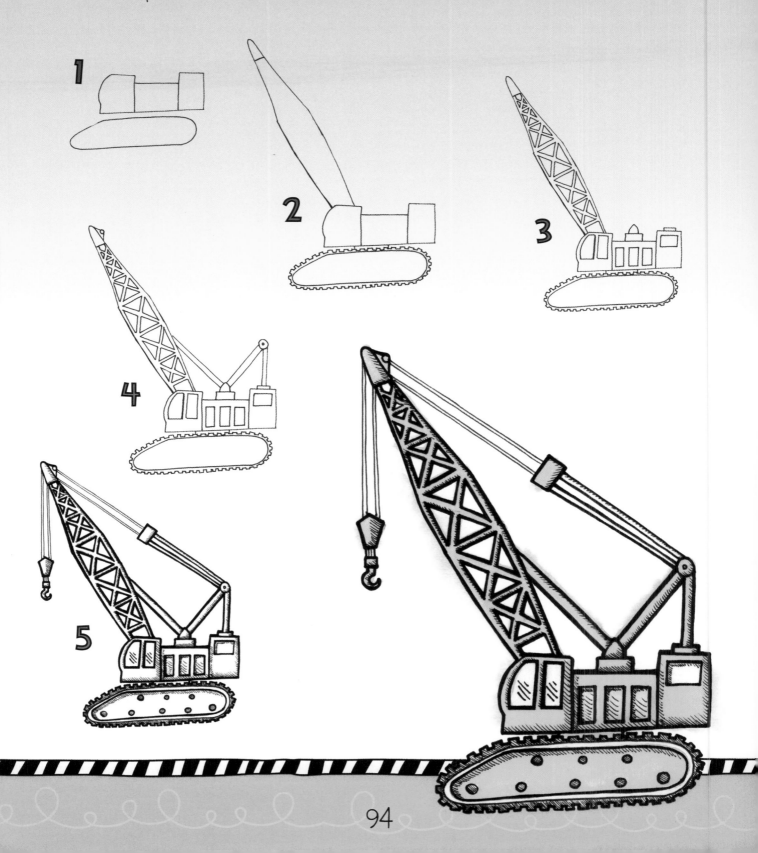

doodle here!

construction zone

Using your crane and the other machines shown on pages 88-89 as inspiration, create your very own construction site on these pages! What are you building?

doodle here!

metal detector

Metal detectors are made up of cool, complex parts. The bottom of the machine hovers along the ground, while a control box in the middle sends signals all the way up the shaft and into the headphones. Are you ready to try your luck at finding buried treasure?

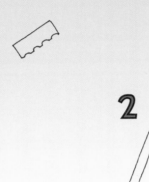

1

2

3

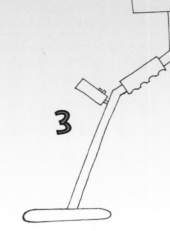

4

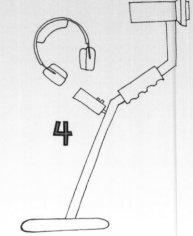

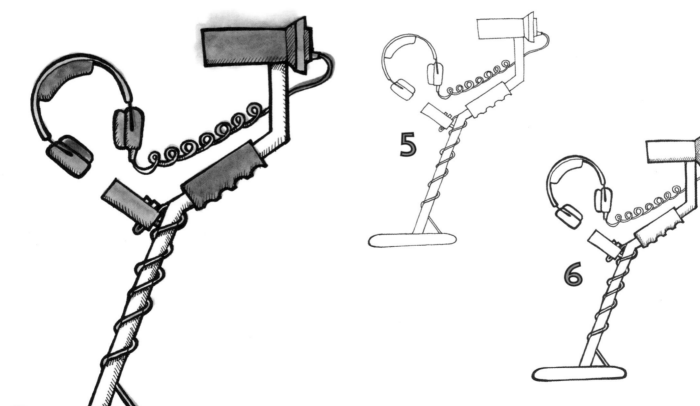

5

6

doodle here!

treasure hunt

Now that your metal detector is ready for use, it's time to put it to work! What shiny, special treasures will you discover in this underground scene?

things in your house

Sometimes you don't need to look any further
than where you live to discover crazy, cool gadgets! This section
shows you some fun everyday things to doodle—from a whirling blender
and a cool clock to a powerful vacuum.

kitchen
tools

cuckoo
clock

blender

toaster

vacuums

hand vacuum

sundial

alarm clock

hourglass

pots

clocks

blender

blenders puree, liquify, and chop food. As you doodle this blender, imagine what delicious things you could make!

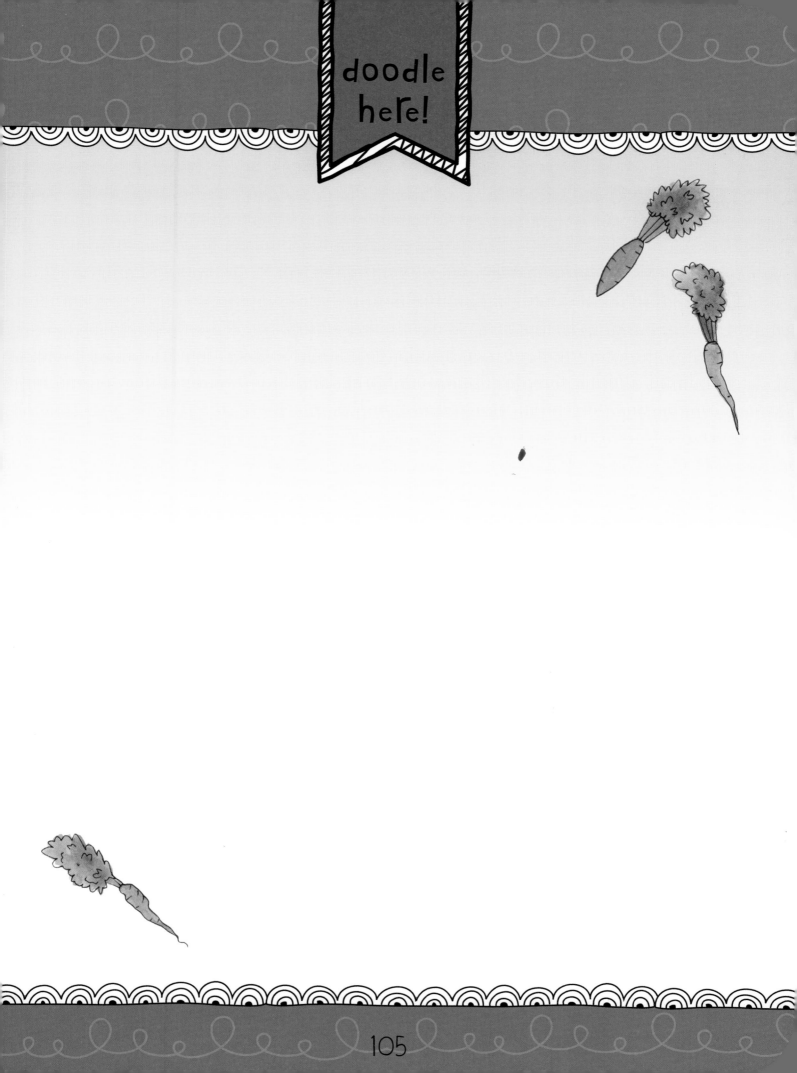

doodle here!

what's cooking?

Imagine you have an entire kitchen full of appliances and ingredients. What would you make to eat? Using the workstation below, doodle your way from start to finish.

tools

Choose a kitchen tool to cook with, and doodle it in the space below.

ingredients

Now add your ingredients!

food

Doodle the delicious food you cooked. Yum!

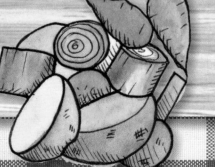

vacuum

Some vacuums are so powerful that they can accidentally suck in stuff from around the house! What ended up in your vacuum that shouldn't be there? Doodle it on the next page.

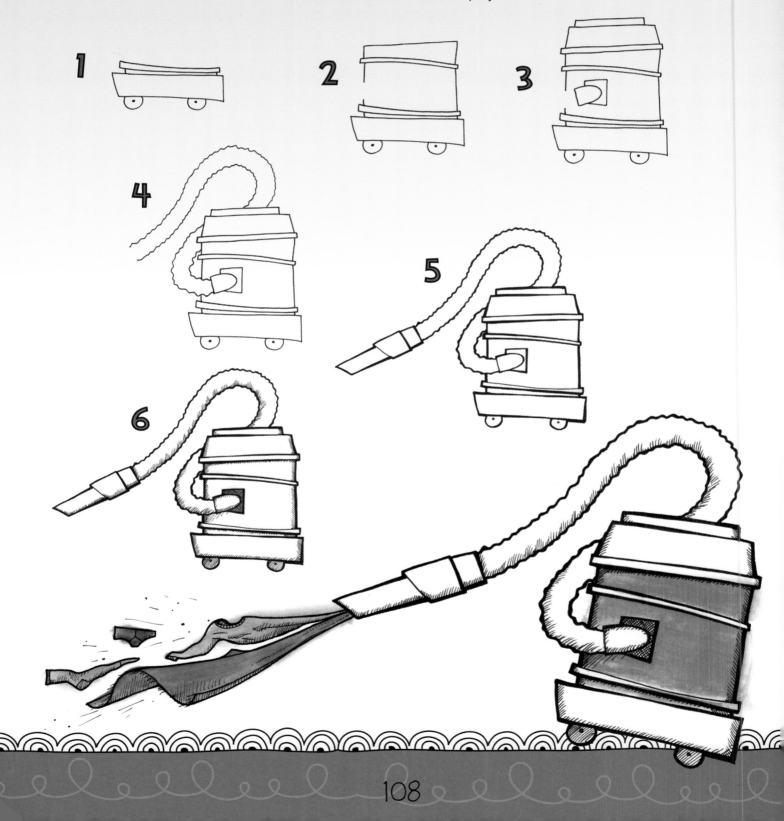

doodle here!

grandfather clock

Clocks come in all shapes and sizes and can be found on the wall, a small table, or even your wrist. How many types of clocks can you think of?
Hint: Check pages 102-103 for some ideas.

1

2

3

4

5

6

doodle here!

cool gadgets

Some of the coolest gadgets are the ones we use for communication and entertainment, such as cell phones, gaming devices, cameras, and computers! In this section you'll find out they aren't just fun to play with—they're fun to doodle too!

vintage camera

instant camera

compass

jigsaw camera

old-fashioned camera

camera on tripod with telescopic lens

twin-reflex camera

multi-lens camera

keyring game

slide phone

walkie-talkies

flip phone

touch screen phone

mp3 player

calculator ruler

portable gaming system

tablet

computer

Thanks to cool electronics like computers, you can talk to friends, play games, search online, and even watch TV by simply pressing a button! Think about the other cool gadgets you like to use as you draw this computer.

doodle here!

camera

People have been capturing memories and telling stories
with photos for more than 100 years! As you draw this camera, think about
the people, places, and things you would take pictures of.

doodle here!

digi-doodles

What's your favorite electronic game to play?
How about your favorite thing to photograph? Doodle them on these pages!

doodle here!

musical things

Music is fun to play and listen to, and it gives us cool subjects to draw. In this section you'll doodle awesome instruments and equipment, and then get ready for your own concert. Rock on!

microphone stand

combination amp

Gibson guitar

electric 12-string guitar

flying V guitar

practice amp

microphone

double neck guitar

headphones

steel guitar

custom guitar

guitar

Every rockstar needs a cool guitar. Imagine you are playing one of your favorite songs, and then rock out with your doodling skills on the opposite page!

doodle here!

dJ table

Officially known as "turntables," DJs use these machines to blend different songs together. The detail in this drawing is really important—each tiny button and knob has a part to play in mixing music!

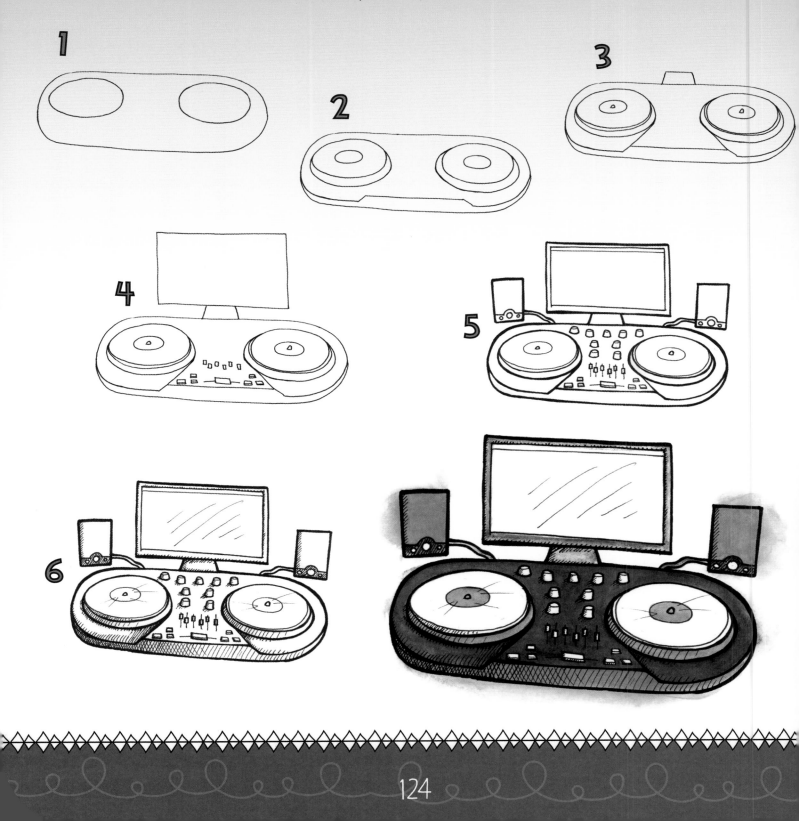

doodle here!

doodle

You are a rockstar!

Combine the musical instruments and equipment you've learned how to doodle into an awesome onstage scene—this is your concert, and the crowd is going wild!

doodle here!

the end

You've learned to doodle everything from a polar bear and a fish to a grandfather clock and a supercool guitar. That might seem like a lot, but there are even more fun things to doodle everywhere you look! You can find inspiration anywhere—at home or school, outside, or from objects right inside your own room. Almost anything can be turned into a fun and silly doodle. This is only the beginning of your doodling adventure!